EXEGESIS

OF

MY SOUL

Epiphany Divine

www.weareaps.com

ISBN: 978-1-945145-93-3

Contact Epiphany Divine:

epiphanydivine@ymail.com

EXEGESIS
OF
MY SOUL

TABLE OF CONTENTS

ACKNOWLEDGMENTS

There are many people I want to thank for making this book possible.

I want to thank my children: Marcus, Marilynn, Joshua, and Shekinah, for always encouraging me to keep moving forward.

I want to thank my siblings: Rosetta, Neretta, Buddy, Jarvis*, Philippa, Nephretaria, for being a major part of my life.

Book cover design:
Lisa Kidder, classmate, and friend

For coaching me, editing, and reviewing my drafts, and formatting my book:
Toneal M. Jackson

*Jarvis N. Caviness (1-25-65 to 3-29-10)

EXEGESIS DEFINED

Exegesis: *(noun),*

exposition; explanation, especially an explanation or critical interpretation of a text; a descendent of the Greek word *exegeisthai,* meaning "to explain" or "to interpret".

"Exegesis." *Merriam-Webster.com Dictionary,* Merriam-Webster, https://www.merriam-webster.com/dictionary/exegesis. Accessed 2 Nov. 2020.

INTRODUCTION

This journey started many years ago. Like most of you, I was introduced to the idea of God at an incredibly young age. Over the years, my understanding of God changed into something other than what my Christian parents and pastors taught me. At an early age, I experienced these encounters that I knew were God. I tried talking about these experiences but was dismissed, viewed as being weird, or even more appallingly called a "witch" by some of my childhood friends. I felt scared and ashamed of these occurrences and stopped talking about them. I tried to continue my life as though these encounters did not occur. As a result, I felt deep depression and anxiety for most of my life.

My life's search for peace has been a constant struggle. Peace eluded me and was always around some proverbial corner. I faced many corners but enjoyed only a few moments of peace. I did not find comfort and did not understand the ways of the world as my Christian upbringing had taught me. I felt that there had to be something wrong with me and that I needed help. I often searched for answers.

While trying to break the cycles of depression and anxiety in my life, I practiced a religious lifestyle. I set and reached many personal and professional goals. For years, I took medications and went to weekly therapy sessions. I found some joy in studying other religions and felt excitement about my new discoveries and ideas. Yet with all my efforts, I did not feel complete or content. Even though I was successful in my nursing career, on the inside I felt like a complete failure. I was unhappy most days but continued to move forward with the hope that a better future would eventually come my way. I developed the mindset of just making it through "this" part of my life and thought that the "next" part would be better for me.

My feelings about my life didn't get better until I stopped suppressing the awareness of my experiences. These encounters with God (as I now call them) provided me with peace and understanding that was beyond the confines of my small world. My experiences are beyond me and anything that my religious leaders could explain. It has taken years for me to unravel the meaning and purpose of these encounters. Now I understand and accept them as a part of my spiritual birthright, which began with an awakening to the Greater that is within me and beyond me. This Greater has been urging me all along toward healing, peace, and purpose.

Today I say, "So what if I see and experience life differently than others? Maybe, this is how I am supposed to see and enjoy life."

By writing, I have only begun to scratch the surface in sharing the details of my experiences. Writing has proven itself to be very therapeutic for me. I often say that writing rights my soul. Words cannot summarize my life experiences and I can never convey the totality of my understanding, but I will try. I feel a strong urge to share my story through poetry. I trust and believe that there are others who will read my poems and relate to what I have written. I make no apologies for what is written here. It is as it is. Thank you for taking the time to read my poetry.

Peace and blessings are yours forever.

LIFE
AND
DEATH

MAMA'S EPITAPH

"Live! Live! Live!
Don't be afraid of facing each day.
Death was here and now is gone.
Today we celebrate!"

With her decisions authenticated
And her wishes fulfilled,
Mama's life was her purpose,
Her soul revealed.

Our inheritance was allotted
And given to us in advance.
She said, "I gave you all that you need.
Don't become selfish after I've passed."

A strange notion, we thought.
At first, we could not see.
A cremation? A memorial service?
It was hard to believe.

She wanted no cards or flowers
Sent with sympathy expressed.
She said, "Tell everyone to donate
To the cause instead."

Her houses, cars, jewels
Were sold and funds given away.
For Mama, you know,
That was her way.

She helped to sick, fed the poor
And volunteered here and there.
Orphaned children were often in our home.
That's how Mama shared.

"Give! Give! Give!
It's more blessed to give than to receive.
The more you give to others,
The richer you will be."

Her list of valuables was simple
For all of us to read:
Her bed, photos, diplomas,
Journals filled with memories,

A clock, a jewelry box,
Videos, CD's,
A cooking pot, an ironing board,
Some plants, her sewing machine,

Her Bibles, her purses,
Handkerchiefs, hats,
Perfumes, some books,
And musical instruments.

She said, "Everything else
Will go to charity.
It is better this way.
In time you will see."

We went through her personal things;
Her toothbrush, toothpaste, and floss,
Her deodorant, lotion, soap,
Her powder and face cloth,

Her comb and brush,
Face cream and make-up too;
These things were more valuable,
Sentimentally tabooed.

She kept no secrets, told no lies.
She always shared the truth.
She said, "I want you all to read my life,
For it is an open book.

Don't live to die,
Die that you might live.
Do your best every day.
Smile with every greeting that you give.

Boys, be a gentleman,
Always be courteous and kind.
Work hard for your families.
Know all your needs, God will provide.

Girls, wear perfume every day,
And always fix your hair, and find
The meaning of your life
And the true beauty that's inside.

Establish your home as a sanctuary,
A haven and a refuge.
As strangers pass your way,
Entertain them with shelter, rest, and food.

Express your heart sincerely,
Always speak the truth.
Write letters to friends, loved ones
And your enemies too.

Take time to replenish
Your body, mind, and soul
Through prayer and meditation,
Solitude and repose.

Laughter is a must!
Learn to laugh and you will survive
Life's turmoils, struggles
And sometimes unfair plights.

Singing and dancing
Are expressions of your soul.
Express yourself!
Be an individual."

Mama was so different
And at times we didn't understand.
To us, she competed with death
As if battling for some gain.

But now that I'm older
And have children of my own,
I'm beginning to understand
The meaning of her song.

You see, the grave had no victory.
Death had lost its sting.
Mama taught us the secret,
Just as Jesus did.

Even though cancer took her body,
It did not destroy her soul.
Mama died long before
And death missed his call.

She said, "I'm not afraid of death anymore.
He can come at any time.
You see, today I live
Because yesterday I died.

Live! Live! Live!
Don't be afraid of facing each day.
Death was here and now is gone.
Today we celebrate!"

WELCOME HOME

When I am gone, release me, and let it be so,
I have things to see and places to go.
You mustn't tie yourself to me with tears.
Be happy that we had many wonderful years.

I gave you love, you can only guess
How much you gave me in happiness!
Thank you for the love you have shown
But now it's time I travel on.

Grieve a while, if grieve you must,
Then let your grief be comforted by trust.
It's only a while that we must part,
Bless and hold our memories in your heart.

Though you can't see or touch me, I'll be near
And if you listen in your heart you'll hear
My love around you, soft and clear
A gentle hug, a whisper in your ear.

I won't be far away, for life goes on.
If you need me, call me; you won't be alone.
And when it's time for you this way to come,
I'll lovingly greet you and say, "Welcome home."

PRECIOUS MOMENTS

That moment just before I die,
I'm certain I am thinking, saying
these words to my children:
> *I loved you as best as I knew.*
> *All we had was moments --*
> *Brief pizza slices of time.*
When I'm gone, know that I
wished for more pizza,
especially breakfast pizza,
leftover kind, microwaved
after being refrigerated overnight,
drinking Kool Aid, watching cartoons
with you, under soft blankets,
snuggling, because we have nothing else
to do, except enjoy and love each other.
Moments, precious moments --
a slice of a lifetime.

EXEGESIS OF MY SOUL

LIFE SUCKS

In life we find this vortex --
the definite, the necessity of death;
do not be afraid; it is life for sure,
with its twisting, sucking, drawing,
alluring powers -- magic!
And the end?
There is no end, but
renewals and refreshing
journeys beyond...
Life sucks you to death,
and death pushes you,
it pushes you to life.
Make use of it.

THE DEBUTANTE

In a regnal gown of crimson taffeta,
Long white gloves, updo, tiara, pearls,
Smile framed by dimpled cheeks,
Soft eyes, charming grace,
She came to me.

Her voice, a windchime, spoke:
    Dance with me, my child.
This willing child obeyed.
I touched her face, held her hand,
Talked about everything.

My tears tarnished her stately dress
With my love, my words, my woes.
Her embrace, unforgettable, sincere;
Her love answered my pain.
We danced until...

I celebrated that transient moment,
Delighted to be her little child, again.
I never questioned why
This vision came to me -
A dance with my deceased mother.

STUCK

I've run out of sleep
and can't find a remedy,
concoction or cloud
that seduces her to return.
Her gentle hand on my back
comforts me, soothes me.
I'm afraid of being fully awake --
the reality that she will never
awaken with me until
I sleep.

CALI'S DEATH

For Kianna

She was playful, cute, and cuddly,
my pet, who slept with me,
kept me warm at night,
now sleeps alone in the cold earth
without her favorite blanket and toys.
Daddy buried Cali in the backyard;
he built a fire and burned
her food, toys and blanket.
The fire kept her warm that night.
The next day
I covered that small pile of dirt
with my favorite blanket,
and tucked the edges into the ground
with big rocks;
Daddy helped me.
He knew I wanted her to stay warm.

A MAN AT THE PARK

A man sat on a park bench
with constipated anger
smeared on his face:
flared horse nostrils,
tightened ostrich lips,
bulging frog eyes,
rouged cheeks,
and a noose of engorged veins
laced around his neck.
Later, he was found
beneath that same park bench;
the trapdoor gave away.

DEATH ON A HARLEY

Are you afraid of Death?
Why? I'm not.
He is my friend.
We met a long time ago.
From time to time he visits me
and we catch up and exchange details
about our experiences since our last
encounter.
Yep! Death lives…
He taught me a lot about myself
and my relationship with Life,
intimate things I never knew.
I am well acquainted with Death.
He is a cool dude.
No tats, no piercings, clean fingernails.
He wears leather chaps and boots
and rides a Harley Davidson on full throttle.
He prefers the manmade beast
and the hum of its smooth machinery.
It soothes his soul.
Yep! Death has a soul.
We ride together sometimes,
no helmet at all, free.

He shared his family secret with me,
his genealogy, his family tree.
He has a lot of cousins, too many to name.
But his distinguished tactics stood out -
Homicide, Suicide, Genocide,
Epidemic, Pandemic, Famine and War.
He has a twin sister, born at the exact same
time.
She gets a lot of presents, celebration, and
joy;
but he gets rage, tears, and sadness.
He is used to it now, but at first he was hurt.
Death is kind and compassionate.
He brings comfort and peace to many.
He is the portal to Life's next cycle
awaiting on the other side.
The twins play
this game every day.
She tosses to him
and he,
he always tosses back.

ACCEPTANCE

ANACONDA

My writhing life:
hurl it to the ground
and choke it into submission,
while the patient, black water
moccasin watches and waits.

DEE

She only plays with me
while everyone sleeps;
she likes sweets more than me,
but I eat everything she eats.
We fight when I read and write,
or try to leave her alone,
like when I think my own thoughts
and plan my escape.
She is always here,
always hanging around.
I try to escape again,
but we share DNA.
Dee is miserable all the time;
she loves to share her misery with me.
I don't like her company,
instead of her sweets,
I eat fluoxetine.

THE FIGHT

Sticks and stones
may break my bones,
but late at night
words comfort me.
Fight with words,
not with hate,
gentle fists manipulate,
twisting fate.

THE OTHER GRAND CANYON

I adore this monument --
open airy spaces, intertwining layers,
possibilities, randomness, impulsiveness,
eccentricities, and precise clarities.

I see its vibrant colors.
I hear its rich sounds.
I inhale its delicious vapors.
Why, it's full of life!

Yet this relic
splashes diluted colors,
bewails muffled sounds,
secretes lethal toxicities.

I perceive the fault line in its skull,
the hidden fracture of its soul --
a fossilized mind,
a carbonized indignity.

NEEDING MORE

Tick tock clocks
ding dong bells
turns the key
opens the door
tilts sideways
it needs
more of itself
to complete
a single
thought.

HOLOCAUST

Hell is a burning holocaust
where broken philosophies cease;
doctrines are no more;
practices have no value;
Heaven is long gone.
Sound judgment emerges:
Survive!
Survive!
Survive!

DOMICILE

A queen-sized bed on the curb
is elegant until the rain calls.
Once a majestic eyelet spread,
now a rain-soaked home.

Cardboard pieces, wet grass, mud,
dingy covers, an old duffle bag;
duct tape and plastic repairs
her A-framed tarpaulins.

REAL LIFE

Ask the right questions
blue toothpaste in the sink
dirty clothes on the floor
the baby cries at night
the neighbor's new black truck
a cup of hot coffee
snow covers the ground
the telephone rings
a sigh,
answers received.

PSYCHOSIS

I couldn't sleep.
I hadn't slept in a few days.
It was two-something in the morning;
outside, three feet of snow on the ground,
snowing, twenty-three degrees,
howling winds --
a typical Yakima winter storm.

When she asked if I was suicidal,
or if I wanted to hurt someone,
I told Lucinda,
the nice, soft-spoken, professional,
hotline crisis volunteer lady,
my new friend, my only friend,
exactly what I felt like doing:

I felt like going into my garage,
getting my tall ladder and other supplies,
climbing onto my roof,
standing real close to the edge,
until I was ready
to clean the trash and leaves
from my clogged, almost damaged gutters.

She advised me to stay on the phone
with her until the ambulance arrived,
because she called the fire department
to fix my gutters; the ambulance was
in case one of them fell off my roof.
My hospital visit was pleasant;
a dose of quetiapine eased me right to sleep.

A.K.A. "PIP"

They called us Pip, a nickname, I guess;
a small black dot, insignificant unless:

one thousand one,
one thousand two,
one thousand three…

used to enhance pigmentation,
as a mark -- a distinct delineation.

The brand stuck and stood tall
like bold capital letters in print;
recognized alone, in a crowd
and at the beginning
and end of sentences.

PULLING TEETH

I have missing teeth
From poor dental care,
Eating a lot of sweets.
When a tooth hurts,
I see the dentist.
Extractions may cost less,
But in the long run,
They are not cheap.

A SOULFUL BOYCOTT

Stop.
Don't corrupt your soul anymore.
Withdraw from the collusion,
conspiracy theories, rumors, ignorance,
prejudices, stereotypes, news;
spend time with the Divine.
Pray.
Fast.
Be still.
Know.
Bewail your virginity's loss,
the sodomizing of your soul.
Purge.
Think.
Think again.
Wait.
Reconsider your position.
Exhaust all delusions of yourself.
Enjoy holy truth.
Find wisdom.
This is an inward journey,
an inner boycott.

SET FREE

I was slave and dumb,
could not speak my tongue,
did not know my name,
did not know my song.

I was slave in body,
one morning, set free;
my body moved about,
my mind, a root-bound tree.

I was slave to deceit,
truth found and redeemed;
slave no more,
now I think and know.

I am free and speak.
I know my tongue.
I know my name.
I sing my song.

PEACE

AT THE RIVER

I went down to the River and the River said
to me,
"Why do you sit under that tree?
Come a little closer; I have something to say.
You are going to be amazed on this bright,
sunny day."

I got closer to the River and I could not
believe
All the things It was saying to me.
"Splish! Splish!" said the Water in a very
low tone.
And before I knew it, the sound was gone!
"Splash! Splash!" said the Water from high
up stream.
I had to pinch myself. Was this a dream?
"Oh, no!" said the River, "I've been speaking
for a very long time,
But very few people listen to this message of
mine.
You are blessed above others to hear my
voice so clear.
God gave me a message for the whole world
to hear.

I am a source of life for all, the animals and the trees.
God flows through me like a gentle breeze.
So keep coming to the Water. Watch, listen and know
There is a Divine meaning with which I flow.
I've baptized many, but only a few have come back to me.
I've often wondered if the others fulfilled their destiny.
Ask everyone you meet as you walk along your way.
Pray to the Father and He will tell you what to say."

I got out of the River, feeling cleansed on the inside.
God spoke to me that day and my soul was baptized.
I walked away from the River, but the River stayed within,
A Well of Waters bubbling in my soul. My new life did begin.

THE DAY I HEARD
THE SNOW FALL

It was a peaceful encounter
On that cold winter day.
I had heard enough troubles
And wanted to slip away.

I played some music
To help ease my pain,
But the more I listened,
The more I remained the same.

I couldn't take it any longer;
I needed to escape and find
A resting place - a refuge
To put my cares behind.

The weather was so frightful,
But nowhere else I could go.
With my coat, hat and gloves,
I went out in the snow.

I walked and I walked.
Just to get away,
And that is when I listened
To what the snow had to say.

It began to fall so freely
And softly to the ground.
And when I looked closely,
A miracle I had found!

The manner in which the snow fell -
Peacefully, freely, and so slow.
I had never noticed
Its path or its flow.

It flowed from above
So lightly and so free.
Each flake was unique,
As unique as you and me.

Watching the snow fall
Made me feel peaceful inside.
I had found a peaceful place,
A place where I could hide.

Deep from within the snow
I, myself, began to emerge.
I heard so much that day
My energy began to surge.

So deep in the snow I went
On that cold winter day.
I just could not believe
How much the snow had to say!

Now when I find myself
Bogged down with fears and cares,
I listen deep within myself
To find peace from life's snares.

THE EAST

With moist blades beneath her feet
Her heart bleeds to the Source of her
strength.
She faces the east as her forefathers did,
But her neighbors face the west.

Her prayers are but an elongated breath,
"Ah..."
It encapsulates her desires and dreams.
All day she breathes...
She breathes...
She breathes...

When the sun is high above, she pauses.
"Be still and know," she hears.
A rush of energy implodes her doubts.
Yet, she breathes on...
She speaks the ancient tongue.
She follows the ways of Truth.

At the cool of the day, her red blood flows
to the ground
As her enemies beat and stone her beautiful
face and body.

Unable to breathe, she hears an answered
prayer,
"Rest. Be at peace."
She faces the east,
But her enemies face the west.

UBIQUITOUS

An un-birth attempted by some
who knew her sacrifice, innocence, and
don't want to remember her
sculptured stories encased in glass,
untouchable, unthinkable, unbelievable.

Could we master an uncultured world
if she was completely unknown;
her words, art, songs,
wiped out, destroyed, annihilated,
unquoted, unpainted, unsung?

However, pulsating loins generate a hum,
an auspicious hum, a holy hum
hums in secret chambers;
she hovers in dank darkness,
waits to rebirth herself.

Discrete and simple she stands,
walks through my field.
I observe her, commune with her,
learn her songs,
and know that Wisdom can never be undone.

I SEEK

Every day I seek.
I seek my own divine.
When I seek,
I see carnage, murder, savage brutality;
Feel pain, loneliness, despondence;
Smell the stench of putrid waste, foul
dung, cannibal stew;
Hear deep melancholy songs,
Dehumanizing vocals, strung abusive
bondage;
React with cantankerous fear, rage,
bitterness;
I become weary, exhausted, exasperated.
I reach the end of my seeking.
I seek no more.
I give up;
I retreat, leave such work for others.
I am not fit to seek my divine.
I wait.
I pray.
Nothingness consumes me.
In quietness, I know.

I know!
I learn all I need to be divine.
Know, experience, and be.
I am divine.

HIEROGLYPHICS

Life, a kaleidoscope
constricts and dilates --
dancing colorful patterns,
Rosetta-stoned mosaics,
without walls
gyrate everywhere,
messages on puffs of air,
whimsical flights;
heart pulsates, *lub, dub...*
consanguinity --
the orchestrated power of
Being.

A CLOSER LOOK

Look a little closer and you will see
that there is more in life to be.
Look a little closer for love within,
a new life for you will begin.
Look a little closer and you will find
the truth that doesn't bind.
Look a little closer and don't be afraid
of the peace that is heaven-made.
Look a little closer and ease your pain;
focus on the joy that's yours to gain.
Look a little closer at the situation;
fill your heart with great expectation!
Look a little closer and come to know
how easy it is for you to grow.
Look a little closer and find miracles divine,
unfolding rapidly; they're yours and mine.
Look a little closer as the birds sing;
a message to you they will bring.
Look a little closer as the clouds roll away;
they really have a lot to say.
Look a little closer as the rain falls to the
ground;

a cleansing within will be found.
Look a little closer within and see
that there is more in life to be.

A CULTURED BRANCH

Men and women sleep in chairs,
talk on cell phones,
while security reads a book,
the prideful people pack and leave.

Arrive early and get a glimpse
of friendly faces, lively conversations,
dirty fingernails pushing elevator buttons,
long lines around the copy machine,

eating food from secret pockets,
grooming in the bathroom,
clothes hanging on statues,
while the owners adjust their

bags of belongings, sit, rest,
or use the framed artwork as a vanity;
live, colorful culture
growing in a Petri dish!

Eavesdrop on their stories,
understand how they survive:
This underground railroad in plain sight
provides dignity for this broken humanity.

Both gentle and feral people
come for electricity, water, shelter,
books, movies, free internet,
knowledge, and opportunity.

Many books are housed in libraries;
all kinds of stories are there to read,
but the downtown branch is where
the best ones are found.

LIFE OF WORDS

Steel toed feet,
a gang of them walk down the street,
with hardhats on, tools in hand,
they work the job until it's done.
Move mountains, build bridges,
dig ditches, pave roads
with their busy arms and legs,
some with messy hair on their heads.
They have lips that smile and frown,
eyes that see, ears, but they only hear me.
Work until the journey's end;
no one can stop them, not even me.
I see them everywhere,
sometimes it's embarrassing;
in my bed, on my toothbrush,
dancing around my house;
in my car, on my phone,
even climbing power lines;
at the park, the mall, the grocery store,
sitting in my shopping cart.
They are everywhere, everywhere I say!
I can't escape them at all.

All kinds and shapes:
loving, lying, fighting, hateful,
cussing, confusing, peaceful,
encouraging, murdering, truthful.
A galleria, transparent menagerie!
A grandiose display of my artistry!
As water cascades down,
taste the bitter in my mouth;
where is the sweet?
I cannot eat these; woe is me.
I have steel toed lips.
I cannot escape this world of mine.
My words have a life of their own;
they function without me,
and will live after I'm gone.

PERSONIFICATION

Some call me teacher, preacher, prophetess;
Some consider me lost;
Some love me; others hate me.
To me, it matters not.
I am a writer although not exclusively,
But also an onlooker, messenger,
Victim, and sometimes a willing sacrifice,
Who tries to recapture and object or event
Using words, images, metaphors, similes,
Alliterations, tone, and down-right
Craziness - an extension of myself -
Whatever it takes to become
The complete experience,
A flamboyant reenactment,
A depth mastery,
Such that if unpleasant,
The reader takes heed
And never returns;
However, if enjoyable,
Indulges frequently.

THE PEST

Sometimes word phrases
bound in my head, up and down,
buzzing, relentless, vibrating clatter,
worrisome, bitter, angry screech with wings,
filled with violent energy,
thrash around, tear up my peace,
take my sleep, *exhaust* me...

I grip my favorite kaiser blade
with one smooth, swift, swing,
decapitate the unsuspecting pest
slice its carotids wide open,
and spatter its messy, bloody contents
all over my once
spotless, white paper.

A moral, mercy kill,
no more misery --
a poet's work.

THE WRITING SWEATER

During the winter season,
my home office is cold.
Every time I use my portable heater,
the power shuts down.
To warm myself,
I increase the thermostat,
I drink hot coffee and tea,
I wrap a blanket over my lap
and around my legs,
I don socks on my feet,
I wear long sleeves,
but the cold persists;
even my fingers hurt and
the warmth from my breath
is not enough to keep them typing.
This cold is an unwelcome distraction!
Warmth is required to
write and create -- my valid concern.
I feel cheated and challenged.
Charged with nervous excitement,
a.k.a. *Anger,*

I search my winter wardrobe
and find this old sweater;
it is soft, my favorite color,
it has pockets for my cold hands,
and a hoodie to cover my head.
It is perfect.
Mr. Rogers and Mr. Cosby
wear sweaters at work;
even Freddy Kruger has a signature sweater.
Sweaters are incognito,
inconspicuous, intelligent.
Sweaters transform.
I anoint this orange cloak for the task.
I try this precious mantle for a few days,
to my surprise, it keeps me warm
and energizes me.
Like green eggs and ham,
I like it!
The temperature is cold in my home office,
but it doesn't bother me or
hinder my endeavors at all.
I am transformed.
I am a bundled-up Scrooge
hovering over my keyboard,
busy, powerful, creative, and warm.

CORNUCOPIA

Unemployed in ordinary affairs,
Wise men take sabbath on the mount;
Busy work consumes consumers but
Wise men desire solitude, rest,
Peaceful altitude,
To observe life course through the heart,
Understand cosmic flow -
A dynamic movement in all.

A holy rest from turmoil, sweat, gore;
Witness hope, inspire, know,
Share lofty kinship
Which echoes in the vales below.
Enlighten
The depth, width, height of existence,
Unravel superstitions and religions -
Imaginary systematic demises.

On sabbath morns,
Behold and perceive
Footprints of a distant wanderer
Who seeks to understand
The bleating of sheep;

He learns relaxation and peace.

Such is the work of wise men, who deep
In prayer, take sabbatical, peruse, glean
A harvest of heavenly messages
For souls to conceive Spiritual antiquities,
Give birth to children of Truth.

A SOLITARY SOUL

He speaks his gentle mind;
writes his thoughts for others to read.
He listens well, lives alone,
surrounds himself with nature,
and breathes the indigenous air.
He is at peace with all living things,
never disturbs another soul.
He leaves more for others to ponder
about life and living well.

WHEN SADNESS COMES

Sit awhile with sadness
Take it by its hand
Fluff up a spot for it
To sit, or let it stand.
Look it in its eyes,
Deep into its soul.
Search for its purpose,
Its meaning, its goal.
Sadness will speak to us;
It has a lot to say.
Be quiet; pay attention;
It will lead the way.
Ask many questions,
Pause, listen, and know
Perhaps now is the time
to change and grow.
So,
Take all the time you need
The rest of your world can wait.
Sit awhile with sadness
Before it is too late.
Heal your broken heart.
Relieve your suffering and pain;

Ease your troubled mind;
Oh, the peace you will gain!
So,
Sit awhile with sadness,
Allow it to lead the way,
And learn and take heed
To all it has to say.

PRAYER
AND
MEDITATION

PEACE AND GUIDANCE

God, at times I'm not sure
how I see You.
Nevertheless,
I will continue to pray
because I know
that You fully see me.
Grant me peace for this journey
and guide me along the way.
Amen.

A CANDLELIGHT PRAYER

Father of Lights,
As I light this candle in honor of You,
I am reminded that You
called me
to be
a light to this world.
Allow Your light
to shine so bright
upon me
and through me.
I seek to follow Your paths
of love, joy, and peace.
Thank You for Your light
that shines so bright
upon me
and guides me
on my way
every day
Bless others to see this light.
Amen.

MY PRAYER

Dear God, thank You for being here
and helping me to find my way.
I was afraid, lost and hurting.
I felt alone in this world.
You showed me a new way to live;
You shared Your love with me.
You are my True Love,
the only Lover of my Soul.
I want You to know
I love You too.
Thank You for my new life in You.
Amen.

A MORNING MEDITATION

Good morning beautiful sunshine!
What radiant joy you bring my way!
The pleasant sound of your footsteps
and the aria of your voice, a treat.
Much excitement you provide me,
and in solace my heart delights
as I am graced by your warm embrace --
the Shekinah Glory of each new morn.

SOUL WORK: WAITING

I sit with quietness and stillness of mind;
I wait for You.
Utterances flee; meditations increase.
I wait for You.
Externally numb; internally keen.
I wait.
You know why I wait.
Time and eternity are one.
Lord, I sit and wait for You.

THE GARDEN

As I walked in the Garden,
Peace was there and walked with me --
an air so fresh and a gentle breeze.
A melodious score the birds did sing;
I encountered the most beautiful thing.
The fragrances were so sweet to behold.
The purpose of life did unfold.
The most pleasant experience,
the essence untold,
more valuable than silver and gold.
I longed to stay in the Garden,
And have my senses appeased;
a blessing so rich I did receive!

A LISTENING PRAYER

I am praying.

A change is coming.

This change starts in me.

I feel the pressure, it squeezes me.

Good pressure, I believe.

It must be good, because

I believe everything happens, exists,

and moves for my good.

I am humble.

I am quiet.

I wait. I wait. I wait.

It is a gift to wait.

I quietly wait as I inwardly change.

Prayer moves me to meditation - listening,

ears tuned in for that soft peaceful knowing.

Listening…

I am listening, a kind of prayer.

Listening for the answer,

an understanding, a path.

Listening is the work that quiets

my rumbling soul.

I tell myself:

> *Be still, be quiet, and listen.*
> *Hush now... I am listening.*

PURLIEU

A spiritual mind rejuvenates;
walks through whose woods these are.
Behold!
A kerfuffle in the leaves --
two convoluted snakes.

A quiet, observant intruder,
lonely, deep and mysterious,
consummates ideas, inspiration;
with leaves on her boots,
walks home.

MY DESIRE

Be in me
And let me be in thee.
Awaken your desires in me.
Awaken me.
Let me be hope.
Let me be love.
Let me be joy.
Let me be peace.
Let me be compassion.
Let me be patient.
Let me be understanding.
Let me be free to be
All that you are in me.
I accept.
I surrender.
I agree.
Give me to desire to be
Your desire for me.

ONENESS
WITH
GOD

EXEGESIS

Study to show myself approved
by my religious teachers;
at some point,
I must exegete myself.

CARS

Religions are like cars that travel on the roads,
Occasionally, they crash
and passengers get hurt or killed.
If drivers are cautious, courteous, and sober,
all cars can enjoy accident-free travels
and reach their destination safely every time.

GOD'S UNFINISHED BOOK

In God's unfinished book,
a thunderstorm is but a
conclusion to a chapter;
the rainbow symbolizes
the beginning of a new one.

BEYOND RELIGION

We sometimes act like we do God a big favor
When we read and quote the Bible,
pray, sing holy songs,
attend church and feign holiness.
Let's do ourselves a favor.
Get real.
Know who we are.
Express our soul's purpose.
Create life around us;
Share hope.
Replenish the earth with kindness.
Discover the God within and follow.
I think that is better.

MY PATH

The root to love is forgiveness.

The root to forgiveness is acceptance.

The root to acceptance is truth.

Once encapsulated, peace.

In its simplest form, this path is
understood as one.

I can't have one without the other.

I choose love.

I choose forgiveness.

I accept the unchangeable things.

I see truth as it is.

I embrace peace.

I maintain this unity within myself.

This is my path.

HANGOVER

I used to be too religious
trying to be spiritual;
now I am simply spiritual
with a religious hangover.

FAMILY

JC'S RULES

He said,
"Roll the dice,
if you land on a property, buy it,
Put houses or a hotel on it.
Build it up when you first buy it.
Don't wait.
Life is too short.
You must do this before you
give the dice to the next player.
You do not have to own a monopoly
before you build and collect higher rent.
We are gangsters; we do what we want."
This tall Black, handsome man,
my mama's baby's daddy,
shared these rules with us while he curled
the dirty paper money in his hands.
He did not like new money;
it was hard to separate and count
the two five hundreds, two hundreds,
two fifties, six twenties,
five tens, five fives, and five ones...
Fifteen hundred dollars total.

We curled our money too.
We loved our dilapidated box;
a few houses, hotels and tokens fell
out every time we picked it up.
We managed to keep all the pieces.
JC was good at this game;
we played the way he taught us.
One day my oldest brother won.
After that,
JC lost repeatedly,
to my other brother,
then to me, and finally
to my little sister.
He never won after that.
He taught us gangsters well.

THE WORLD TRAVELER

When I first heard the word Impetigo,
I contemplated amazing places
in Brazil, Africa, Australia,
Mexico, France, and Spain --
The kind of places my social studies
teacher made me write about.
You know, and read in front of the class.
My reports were thorough,
an other worldly experience.
In my mind, I went to each place,
beheld the incredible landscape,
enjoyed exotic culture,
and ate exquisite cuisine.

I played new games,
made friends,
wore cultural attire,
danced native dances,
learned to hunt by land and sea,
and spoke foreign languages naturally.
I watched movies without subtitles;

I visited art museums,
slept in a tropical rainforest.
I blended indigenously;
the experience, an international bliss!

While lying on the examining table
and revelling in the glories
of my multicultural pedigree,
I overheard my pediatrician explain
Impetigo to my mother;
That's when I realized
I will never travel there again.

A LEGACY

My heritage gives me identity.

My culture gives me tradition.

My religion gives me a path.

My legacy is what I choose to do with them.

WHY POETRY?

I started writing poetry
Because I did not think I could
Write a book and tell
The whole story.

THE BEST SELLER

I kept telling my children I am a great writer.
They finally believed me when I gave them
Limited, first edition copies of my will.
We discuss the plot of that rare,
Never revised, best seller all the time.

GREATNESS

I sat.
She became
a young lady
strut into life
take her pedestal
proclaim her right
to be known.
It took generations
to create me
to create her.

CHILDREN LIE

Strawberry jelly globs on the counter,
Breadcrumbs on the table,
Peanut butter on his face,
He said he did not eat
A sandwich.
Children lie.
They lie about simple things.

THE UGLY TRUTH

My daddy used to say,
"The truth ain't always pretty.
Truth is an evil spirit with sharp teeth;
it growls and gnaws at your soul.
Adults think they want to know it,
but enlightenment comes at a huge price.
Once on that endless course,
the ugliness exposes their souls.
Have you seen your ugliness?
Be careful little children
of the truth you seek."

TSUNAMI

A small hand drops a pebble in a lake;
Miles away, the ocean swells, moves closer.
We feel a gentle stimulation,
Refuse to believe such agitation
Comes from a little child.

PHILANTHROPY

Some people have a bountiful heart,
give from the nothingness that they possess;
while others who give from stolen property,
think they are blessed.
A true philanthropist gives inspiration
where there isn't any
hope at all;
teaches unfortunate souls how to create
wealth when they only have
a pile of dirt.

HER SOCKS

Her mismatched socks are inside out;
she smiles and struts
into the women's shelter,
with a child holding each hand;
while they sleep, a fire ignites in her --
their brazen flint.

Strangers whisper, point at her
protruding belly, bruised body;
she pays them no mind.
She speaks to her children, they listen:
Look at my provocative socks,
the jagged peaks and valleys,
a bouquet of pine trees.

Their small fingers touch the soft
mountains, follow the colorful
ridges to distant places she describes;
their eyes ablaze, they smile, she
continues:
These repulsive socks hug my feet,
exude vibrant healing energy,
prevent winter's crawl.

In quiet contemplation, they sit.
Her daughter inverts her sweater,
wears it, declares:

I like your style.

Her son puts his shoes on the wrong feet.
Their nuclear laughter mushrooms in the
air;

a pyrogenic shield surrounds them.

I REMEMBER

Whenever I hear a choo-choo train
Blowing on its horn,
I think of being over Grandma's house
And playing in her yard.
I remember sitting in Grandpa's chair
And watching TV with him.
He liked to watch baseball games
And old black and white movies.
Even though our church was near
A steel plant and I didn't like the smell,
I enjoyed going because
All of my family went there.
I remember my favorite baby doll;
Her name was Christy Lee.
She wore a blue dress
With white lace around the hem.
My favorite book was about a bird
Who was looking for his mom.
I was glad when finally, she was found.
I remember riding the yellow bus to school
And the smell of the seats,
The bouncing up and down

And the breaks that squeaked.
While on the school playground,
I went from the swings to the slide,
But my favorite of all
Was the merry-go-round.
I remember our family gatherings,
And all the fun we used to have.
It was like a great feast was going on
With all the food that we shared.
Now that I'm grown up
With children of my own,
I remember my childhood
Yesteryears with the sound of that horn.

CAN COCKROACHES HEAR?

I often wonder if cockroaches can hear.
I wonder if they hear when my
breadcrumbs fall on the counter
or other foodstuff dropped as bait.
I wonder if they smell my food
when I start cooking
and if they know exactly when it's done,
timing their arrival for when I sit and eat,
so they can eat in peace too?
Are they smart like that?
I know they scatter
when the lights come on.
I know they move fast
when they feel vibrations
from my footsteps.
I don't light up like that
or move sharply when I watch them.
My cockroaches must be blind.
Yep, blind for sure.
In fact, I know they are blind,
because they come out from hiding,
even though the light is on,

and I stand here waiting for them
with a can of Raid in my hand.
Dumb, blind, dead bugs.

IN THE SHOWER

This morning when I took my shower,
I discovered I was not alone.
I did not sing as usual;
Water wanted to sing his song.

I listened as he sung his solo
With such passion and intensity.
He had such a strong and powerful voice.
I was mesmerized by his vocal ability.

Washcloth and Soap got my attention,
By waving their arms and legs at me.
It was their turn to sing along.
They sang in perfect harmony!

Washcloth and Soap made beautiful
melodies,
Then Soap sat down and hummed the rest,
Washcloth took the lead and sang.
Intimately, she knew me best.

Water's voice became scratchy and hoarse.
The heat began to leave his flow.

He said, "I will sing to you another time,
But right not, I must go."

I stood there saddened by the news
And longed to hear them sing to me once more.
Then, to my surprise,
Someone knocked on the shower door.

I said, "I want to be left alone
And finish my shower privately,
This is my special time.
I want to spend it only with me!"

The knocking continued,
He was persistent and waited patiently.
I gave in, opened the door and saw
Towel, waiting to dance with me.

MAMA'S COOKING

She had the rhythm in her hands
And the melody in her heart.
Her music book was sometimes used
To make sure the instruments
Did their part.

Her kitchen was filled with music
When the pots and utensils sang.
She was the conductor
Of the most beautiful scores.
This was her worship,
The thing she truly adored.

Fried chicken, pork chops,
Barbecue ribs and rolls,
Green beans, mashed potatoes,
Banana pudding and yams
Were some of the dishes prepared
By this master musician.

LOVE

LOVER OF MY SOUL

A kiss with the passion of Your being,
so sweetly I am receiving.
You are forever here with me;
with another I cannot be!
Where can I go, and You not follow?
For You are my hopes and dreams of tomorrow.
A quiet moment in the night
fills with pleasure and delight.
Because of You my heart is content
with the time we have spent.
Growing stronger and wiser
each and every day,
I know You are here to stay.
You wipe away all my tears;
You comfort me through the years.
To come to know You is my goal,
for You are the Lover of my Soul.

THE ESSENCE OF YOU

A slow, smooth stride,
sensuous smile, sweet kiss,
warm embrace, delicate touch,
a new day awakens my soul,
full of passion,
and ultimate fulfillment,
kindness, thoughtfulness,
generosity;
Loyalty is Your strength,
Privacy is Your specialty.
As the sun sets, You appear;
as the flowers bloom,
my soul yields to You.
Your movement moves me,
take possession of me;
I am all that I am because
of the essence of You.

LOVE CALLS

Love calls...
Will I answer?
I hold my breath and take one step.
Darkness grips my heart, causes me to
plunge
Into the depths of uncertainty.
How long will I wonder, question?
Undoubtedly, my whole life.

I am inside and feel strange.
I move into another.
Leaving myself behind, I must find
Hidden treasures that lie within you.
My expectations are lost, but I have found
That secret place - the hidden garden of
my beloved.
Yet, Love bids me further,
Continues to call me.
Why bother me with such ideas?
All is lost.
You continue to call and awaken me during
the night.

Finding no rest, I sit and listen to the truth
of your story.
I become brokenhearted and weep.
I reach out to you, but your treasures are
gone.
Then why call me? Why trouble me thus?

Love calls...
Will you answer?
Hold your breath and take that step.
Allow darkness to grip your heart and
plunge
Deep into despair.
Be lost my Love.
Be lost forever in me
As I am lost in You.

SLEEP MATE

With whom do I sleep?
He marinates my flesh all night long,
Whispers in my ears,
Body parts penetrate my dome
Reveals my life as a tortured soul.
I enter the hall of shame,
Where thoughts push the limits of my mind,
Move me into a space and time
To accomplish fate.
Fluffy pillows, comfy sheets, warm downs
On cold wintry nights
Bind me to these unbeatable charms.
This bedfellow creeps in my room and lurks
In the shadows at my windowsills,
Reveals one puzzle piece at a time,
Lead me on a path that never ends.
I slumber with him all night long.
This beguiling bedfellow bethinks me a fool!
I cry, cry, cry
To be released from this cacophony.
I hear a voice deep within my soul
Tell me the path to take and push forward.

I move to a simple motif,
A single-minded belief:
I am that I am is what I am to be!
I am a precious treasured eternity.
I sleep alone at night.
I sleep with me.

A LOVE SO NEAR

I have heard of a Love so true,
    But I can't even seem
To understand this Love so true
    I am away from You, Love.

I've never had a Love like this,
    So near and yet so far.
Then why can I not come to You
    And tell you how I feel, Love?

So why can I not share this Love?
    I am so much afraid.
I am afraid that You will not
    Return this Love to me, Love.

I don't know how or where to start
    To tell You how I feel.
So I must keep this Love to myself,
    So far away from You, Love.

You'll never know the way I feel
    And think of You each day.
A Love so deep inside my heart
    Safe from sorrow and pain, Love.

This is the way that it must be
    To keep this Love alive.
A Love so near and yet so far
    For You inside my heart, Love.

I've never had a Love like this,
    So near and yet so far.

OUR FORM

We are born spiritual
and we die spiritual;
all that happens between
life and death is spiritual.
Smooth as curves in this world,
our clay mold takes shape.
Fiery winds purify,
but our form never breaks.
Our form never breaks.

THIS PLACE

I am here;
You are there.
We are together
in this place.
I am there;
You are here.
We are in this place.
I am.
You are.
We are this place.

FLAMES

A shish-kabob
meat on meat
cooking delicious smells
burning oneness
juices marinating
pleasures oozing
day and night
we consume.

THE BULL'S EYE

Your gun is cocked and loaded!
Your solitary goal is in sight;
with accuracy and precision,
you pull the trigger tight
and hit the center
of her pink bull's eye.

1:35AM

Feeling pretty good
Sitting at the kitchen table
Playing cards with my sisters
Sipping my favorite drink
Dancing to the music
Singing right along
Kicking it with friends
And hanging out until dawn.
Feeling really good!
Remembering...
Remembering time spent with him
Wishing he was here
Longing for him deeply
Missing him
Wanting him
Feeling pretty lonely.

TREASURES

Treasured treasures,
shared great wealth,
cherished forever,
placed in a chest.
Rare jewels we've found,
our precious stones,
lost to others,
for us alone.
Memories of great wealth,
relationship profound,
Sacred, peculiar,
uniquely ours.

AN AFFAIR, ALMOST

If you only knew,
were his words to me.
If you only knew,
were my words to him.
We both knew.
The look, we
opened secret chambers;
the lust, we
yearned and burned
for each other;
the passion, we
allowed one touch,
then quietly, gently, we
pulled away --
our private orgasm
was to do nothing.
We both knew,
but did nothing.
We reduced ourselves
to knowing,
just knowing.

THE BEST DOUGHNUT

In my hand
I hold this fresh baked delight;
honey colored crusted bun
glazed in a white coat of
gooey goodness,
perfect sweetness,
and warm softness.
My glands stand
and applaud
its arrival.
My mouth is ready
to indulge my pleasure.
I deliciously
watch as I
slowly
drop
it on
the
bitter,
chocolate,
cold,
dirty
ground.
A fresh baked waste!

STAINS ON HIS MIND

He said,
I have no control of my mind
When it comes to you.
Do you think I can get rid of
you
By seeing a shrink?
What happened between
Us is deep in my
subconscious,
The effects sustain all of me,
All of my conscious needs.
You are the stain on my
favorite shirt
I washed it many times.
When I wear this scarlet
letter,
My friends stare at me
for a few seconds,
But comment no more.
They know.

WINDOW TO MY SOUL

For Lamine

While I wash dishes,
wait for the tea kettle to whistle,
and talk to my boyfriend,
he says, "Take a pic of yourself and send it
to me."
My French-speaking boyfriend, in Côte
D'Ivoire,
often asks me to take a "pic" and send it to
him.
Today is different for me.
After yesterday's dark overcast,
today's sunlight reigns and reveals
Nature's panoramic opus.
While I stand at that kitchen sink,
I look through the partially opened window.
I hear enchanted birdsongs.
I smell the wet earth and lavender blossoms.
This invitation:
The full green grass beneath my feet,
The trees along the edge of the property line,

The entryway,
The zephyr,
Sweet Tranquility.
I want him to experience this moment.
I set my cellphone on the windowsill
and take two pictures -
one of myself and the other of my view.
I send both.
I wait for his response.
He comments on one.
He says, "Your eyes reflect peace, mon amour."
I breathe deeply.
He continues, "Oui! I see the forest deep in
your eyes!"
I sigh completely.
I explain to him that I was
walking through the woods
when I took that picture.

WHAT LOVE IS

Let me tell you what love is.

You want money in your pocket, work for it.

You want to drive a nice car, work for it.

You want a house to live in, work for it.

You want a relationship to last, work for it.

Love is work.

Work on loving yourself.

Work on loving others.

Work your love until it works.

Love is the work that gets the job done.